Secrets We Keep

The Psychology of Deception in Love

Nail Taylor

Lost Love Gone Bonkers

DEDICATION

Dedicated to my darling sister Nadine
Burdens of the heart took you from us
Let me help your memory last

Table of Contents

Understanding Deception in Relationships

The Nature of Deception

Deception is a multifaceted phenomenon that often serves as the bedrock of extramarital affairs. At its core, deception entails a deliberate distortion of the truth, whether through outright lies, omissions, or misrepresentations. In the context of emotional affairs, individuals may find themselves crafting elaborate narratives to justify their actions or to shield their partners from the painful reality of their choices. This tendency to deceive is not merely a reflection of moral failings; rather, it is deeply rooted in psychological mechanisms that navigate the complexities of human relationships. Understanding these mechanisms is crucial for individuals entangled in emotional affairs, as it helps them confront the underlying motivations that drive their behavior.

The motivations behind deception in extramarital relationships are varied and often intertwined. Many individuals engage in emotional affairs to fulfill unmet needs within their primary relationship, such as emotional intimacy, validation, or excitement. In doing so, they may rationalize their deceit by convincing themselves that their actions are justified, either as a response to their partner's shortcomings or as a means of self-preservation. This cognitive dissonance allows them to maintain a façade of integrity while simultaneously engaging in behavior that contradicts their values. By exploring these motivations, individuals can gain clearer insight into their actions and the impact of deception on their emotional well-being.

Emotional connections formed outside of marriage often thrive in an environment of secrecy and misrepresentation. The thrill of an affair can create an intoxicating bond, one that is often intensified by the shared experience of deception. Couples engaged in such relationships may find themselves investing heavily in their emotional connections, crafting elaborate stories to explain their absences or to mask their true feelings. However, this reliance on deception can lead to an escalation of emotional investment, complicating their lives further. The emotional high derived from secrecy can be addictive, making it increasingly difficult to detach from the affair, even as the risks and consequences become more apparent.

Moreover, the role of deception extends beyond the individuals directly involved in the affair. Often, the web of lies expands to include friends, family, and even co-workers, creating a complex network of false narratives that can ensnare multiple lives. For those involved, maintaining this network becomes a burden that weighs heavily on their conscience. The psychological toll of living a double life can lead to anxiety, guilt, and a pervasive sense of isolation. Recognizing the broader impact of deception not only encourages individuals to reflect on their own behavior but also highlights the potential harm inflicted on others, further complicating their emotional landscape.

Ultimately, understanding the nature of deception in the context of extramarital affairs is essential for anyone involved in such relationships. By examining the psychological underpinnings of their actions, individuals can begin to untangle the web of lies they have woven and confront the reality of their choices. This process of introspection can lead to significant personal growth, allowing individuals to reassess their motivations and the consequences of their actions. In doing so, they can find a path toward greater emotional honesty, whether that leads to mending their primary relationship or making the choice to pursue a new direction in life.

Types of Deception in Romantic Contexts

In the intricate landscape of romantic relationships, deception plays a pivotal role, particularly in the context of extramarital affairs. Understanding the various types of deception is essential for individuals navigating these complex dynamics. Deceptive behaviors can range from benign white lies to more malicious forms of manipulation, each serving distinct psychological functions. These deceptions often arise from a desire to protect oneself, maintain relationships, or fulfill unmet emotional needs, shedding light on the motivations behind extramarital connections.

One prevalent type of deception in romantic contexts is emotional deception, which often manifests in emotional affairs. In these scenarios, individuals may misrepresent their emotional availability or the depth of their feelings. They might present themselves as wholly committed to their spouses while simultaneously cultivating a deep emotional bond with someone outside the marriage. This form of deceit is particularly insidious, as it can create an illusion of intimacy that allows individuals to justify their behaviors to themselves and others. The emotional connections formed outside of marriage often fill voids left by unmet needs, creating a cycle of deception that is difficult to break.

Another significant type of deception is contextual manipulation, where individuals selectively share truths to create a favorable narrative about their extramarital involvement. This can include embellishing stories about their spouse's shortcomings or downplaying the significance of their extramarital partner. By controlling the context in which their actions are perceived, individuals can alleviate feelings of guilt or shame associated with their affairs. This manipulation not only serves to protect the relationship but also enables the deceiver to maintain a positive self-image, often rationalizing their actions as necessary for personal happiness.

Additionally, there is social deception, which entails misleading others about the nature of one's relationships. Individuals engaged in extramarital affairs may craft elaborate stories to explain their absences or to account for suspicious behavior. This can involve lying to friends, family, or even the extramarital partner about their circumstances. Social deception not only complicates the lives of those involved but also creates a web of lies that can lead to greater emotional turmoil and anxiety. The fear of exposure often fuels further deception, trapping individuals in a cycle that becomes increasingly difficult to escape.

Lastly, self-deception plays a crucial role in the psychology of cheating. Individuals may convince themselves that their actions are justified or that their emotional needs are legitimate, even when they recognize the potential harm to their spouse. This internal rationalization allows them to disengage from the moral implications of their choices, fostering a sense of entitlement to seek fulfillment outside their marriage. Understanding these types of deception is vital for individuals involved in extramarital affairs, as it can lead to greater self-awareness and, ultimately, more informed decisions about their relationships. Recognizing the psychological underpinnings of these deceptions can encourage a deeper exploration of motivations and desires, paving the way for healthier emotional connections in the future.

The Psychological Impact of Lies

The act of lying, particularly within the context of extramarital affairs, has profound psychological implications that extend far beyond the immediate consequences of the deception itself. For individuals engaged in emotional affairs, the lies can create a complex web of feelings and behaviors that distort reality. These falsehoods often serve as a mechanism to justify the affair, allowing individuals to compartmentalize their emotions and maintain a semblance of normalcy in their primary relationship.

However, the psychological toll of this deception can lead to significant internal conflict, guilt, and anxiety, as the individual grapples with the disparity between their actions and their values.

Lies in the context of infidelity can foster a false sense of security. Those involved in emotional affairs may convince themselves that their deceit is harmless or even justified, believing that they are simply seeking fulfillment that is lacking in their primary relationship. This rationalization can create an illusion of control, as they navigate the complexities of two relationships. However, this illusion is precarious, often leading to deeper feelings of dissatisfaction and disconnection. As the individual becomes entangled in the lies, they may experience a deterioration of their self-esteem, as the recognition of their deceit clashes with their self-image and moral compass.

The emotional connections formed outside of marriage are often built on a foundation of secrets and lies. While these connections may initially feel exhilarating and liberating, they are frequently accompanied by underlying anxieties about exposure and judgment. The psychological impact of maintaining such a façade can be overwhelming. Individuals may find themselves oscillating between moments of passion and guilt, creating a cycle of emotional highs and lows. This instability can complicate their emotional landscape, leading to increased stress and anxiety as they try to navigate their dual lives without revealing their truth.

Furthermore, the lies that individuals tell themselves and others can lead to a distorted perception of love and intimacy. In extramarital affairs, the emotional intimacy developed with a partner outside of marriage can create an illusion of a deeper connection, often leading to misguided beliefs about true love and fulfillment. This distortion can prevent individuals from addressing the underlying issues in their primary relationship, as they become preoccupied with the excitement of the affair rather than confronting their dissatisfaction at home. Consequently, the cycle of deception not only harms the individuals involved but also perpetuates a cycle of emotional disconnection in both relationships.

Ultimately, the psychological impact of lies in the context of extramarital affairs underscores the importance of honesty and transparency in relationships. While the allure of deception may seem enticing, it often leads to a greater sense of isolation and emotional turmoil. For those engaged in emotional affairs, recognizing the psychological ramifications of their actions can be a crucial step toward healing and self-discovery. By confronting the lies and the motivations behind them, individuals can begin to untangle the complex emotions at play, paving the way for more authentic connections and a deeper understanding of their own needs and desires.

Emotional Affairs: A New Kind of Connection

Defining Emotional Affairs

Emotional affairs represent a complex and nuanced form of infidelity that extends beyond mere physical attraction or sexual encounters. These affairs are characterized by deep emotional connections formed outside the boundaries of a committed relationship. Unlike traditional affairs, where the primary focus may be on sexual interaction, emotional affairs thrive on intimacy, companionship, and shared vulnerabilities. Partners in such relationships often find themselves confiding in someone who provides a sense of understanding and support that they may not be experiencing within their marriage. This emotional bond can become a crucial aspect of the affair, leading to a significant psychological investment that complicates the dynamics of both the extramarital relationship and the primary partnership.

The motivations behind emotional affairs are varied and often rooted in unmet needs within the primary relationship. Individuals may seek out emotional connections when they feel neglected, unappreciated, or emotionally disconnected from their spouse. The search for validation, intimacy, or excitement can drive someone toward another person who seems to offer the understanding and attention they crave. This pursuit of emotional fulfillment can sometimes feel justified, as the individual may believe they are merely seeking solace rather than engaging in betrayal. However, this rationalization does not negate the underlying issues of trust and commitment that are essential to a healthy marriage.

Psychologically, emotional affairs can be both liberating and damaging. They provide an escape from the pressures and discontent of a primary relationship, allowing individuals to explore different aspects of themselves and their desires. This newfound emotional freedom can offer a sense of empowerment and fulfillment. However, it often comes at a steep cost, as the deception involved in maintaining such an affair can lead to feelings of guilt, shame, and internal conflict. The emotional turmoil that arises from living a double life can be profound, creating an ongoing cycle of secrecy that further erodes the individual's sense of self and their primary relationship.

The role of deception in emotional affairs cannot be overstated. Maintaining a façade requires constant lying and manipulation, which places strain on both the individual and their legitimate partner. The secrets kept to protect the affair can lead to a breakdown of trust and communication in the primary relationship, setting the stage for potential emotional devastation. Moreover, the person engaged in an emotional affair may struggle with the fear of discovery, which can create a heightened sense of anxiety and instability in their life. This deception not only affects the individuals directly involved but also casts a shadow on the larger family unit, affecting children and extended relatives who may be unaware of the underlying issues.

Ultimately, understanding emotional affairs requires a deep dive into the psychological aspects of human connection and the nature of commitment. Individuals engaged in such affairs must confront the reasons behind their choices and the consequences those choices carry. The complexity of emotional affairs challenges the traditional notions of infidelity, urging a reevaluation of how we perceive loyalty and love. By examining the emotional needs and psychological motivations that fuel these relationships, individuals can begin to unravel the secrets they keep and potentially find a path toward healing, whether that means addressing the issues within their marriage or deciding to pursue a different direction in their lives.

The Psychological Needs Behind Emotional Affairs

Emotional affairs, distinct from physical infidelity, often arise from unmet psychological needs within a primary relationship. Individuals engaged in these clandestine connections frequently seek emotional fulfillment that may be lacking at home. This pursuit is driven by a complex interplay of factors, including a desire for intimacy, validation, and understanding that the primary relationship fails to provide. Recognizing these psychological motivations is vital for those involved in emotional affairs, as it sheds light on the deeper issues at play and offers a pathway to understanding their actions and emotions.

At the core of many emotional affairs is a profound sense of loneliness or disconnection. When partners in a long-term relationship become complacent or fail to nurture their emotional bond, one or both may feel neglected. This vacuum can lead individuals to seek companionship outside their marriage, where they often find someone who appears to listen, empathize, and validate their feelings. The allure of being truly seen and heard can be intoxicating, making the emotional affair seem like a refuge from the isolation felt within the primary relationship.

Additionally, the need for validation plays a significant role in driving individuals toward emotional affairs. When partners feel unappreciated or undervalued in their marriages, they may turn to someone outside the relationship who offers praise and affirmation. This external validation can temporarily boost self-esteem and create a sense of worth that is lacking at home. However, this strategy often leads to a cycle of dependency on the emotional affair for validation, further complicating the individual's emotional landscape and making it increasingly difficult to address the underlying issues within their primary relationship.

Moreover, unresolved personal issues and past traumas can heavily influence the decision to engage in an emotional affair. Individuals may seek solace in relationships that reflect their unresolved conflicts or unmet needs from earlier life experiences. These emotional connections can become a means of coping with feelings of inadequacy, abandonment, or rejection. By exploring these psychological underpinnings, individuals can better understand their motivations and the patterns that lead to emotional infidelity, ultimately providing insights necessary for personal growth and healing.

Lastly, the role of deception cannot be overlooked in the context of emotional affairs. The act of hiding feelings and experiences from a spouse often creates an intricate web of lies that can further entangle those involved. While deception may initially serve as a protective mechanism to preserve the primary relationship, it ultimately contributes to feelings of guilt, anxiety, and shame. Understanding the psychological needs that drive the need for secrecy can clarify the dynamics of emotional affairs, allowing individuals to confront their choices and seek healthier ways to fulfill their emotional needs without resorting to deception. By addressing these psychological aspects, individuals can work towards rebuilding their primary relationships or finding more authentic connections that satisfy their emotional requirements.

The Difference Between Emotional and Physical Affairs

In the realm of extramarital relationships, distinguishing between emotional and physical affairs is crucial for understanding the complexities of infidelity. While both types of affairs can cause significant harm to a marriage, they manifest in different ways and stem from various underlying motivations. An emotional affair centers on the development of deep emotional connections with someone outside of the marriage, often characterized by intimacy, affection, and a sense of companionship. In contrast, a physical affair typically involves sexual encounters and physical intimacy without necessarily fostering an emotional bond. Recognizing these distinctions can help individuals navigate their feelings and the consequences of their actions.

Emotional affairs are often rooted in unmet needs within a primary relationship. Individuals engaged in such affairs may seek validation, support, or understanding that they find lacking in their marriage. This desire for emotional connection can lead to a profound bond with another person, one that may feel more fulfilling than the original partnership. The psychological aspects of emotional affairs are significant; they often involve sharing secrets, fostering intimacy, and developing a sense of trust that can rival or even surpass that found in the primary relationship. Such connections can create feelings of excitement and passion, as partners may feel understood and valued in ways they do not experience at home.

On the other hand, physical affairs are frequently driven by a different set of motivations.

They may arise from a desire for novelty, adventure, or sexual fulfillment that is perceived to be absent in the marriage. In these cases, the affair may be more about physical attraction and gratification, with emotional ties being secondary or even non-existent. This type of infidelity can often be easier to compartmentalize, as the individual may convince themselves that engaging in physical intimacy with someone else does not inherently threaten their emotional bond with their spouse. However, the consequences of a physical affair can still be profound, often leading to feelings of guilt, shame, and further deception.

The role of deception in both emotional and physical affairs cannot be overstated. Individuals involved in either type of affair often engage in a web of lies, hiding their actions from their spouses and carefully curating their lives to maintain the façade of normalcy. This secrecy can create significant psychological stress, as the individual grapples with the duality of their life. In emotional affairs, the deception may be more about concealing the depth of the connection, while in physical affairs, the focus may be on hiding the act of infidelity itself. This continuous act of lying can erode the self-esteem of those involved, leading to a cycle of further deceit and emotional turmoil.

Ultimately, understanding the differences

between emotional and physical affairs is essential for individuals in extramarital situations. Recognizing the motivations behind these affairs can facilitate a deeper understanding of personal needs and desires, as well as the impact of infidelity on all parties involved. By exploring the psychological aspects that drive these behaviors, individuals can begin to confront their own actions, understand the complexity of their emotions, and make informed decisions about their relationships. Acknowledging these distinctions can also pave the way for healing, whether that involves reconciliation with a spouse or a re-evaluation of one's own emotional and physical needs in future relationships.

The Motivations for Cheating

Psychological Triggers of Infidelity

Psychological triggers of infidelity are complex and multifaceted, often rooted in emotional, relational, and individual psychological factors. Individuals engaged in extramarital affairs frequently cite feelings of dissatisfaction in their primary relationships as a significant catalyst for seeking intimacy outside of marriage. This dissatisfaction can stem from various sources, including unmet emotional needs, lack of communication, or a sense of stagnation in the relationship. When partners fail to address these issues, one or both may subconsciously seek validation or excitement elsewhere, leading to emotional affairs that blur the lines of commitment and loyalty.

Another psychological trigger is the allure of novelty and excitement. Humans are inherently drawn to new experiences and the thrill of the unknown; this is particularly potent in romantic contexts. The initial stages of a relationship often involve intense passion and a sense of adventure, which can diminish over time in long-term partnerships. For some individuals, the desire to recapture this exhilarating feeling can lead them to seek out extramarital connections. Emotional affairs often provide a temporary escape from the routine and predictability of a long-term relationship, making infidelity appealing to those who yearn for excitement and variety.

Emotional disconnection within the primary relationship can also serve as a significant psychological trigger for infidelity. When partners feel distant or disconnected, one may seek emotional intimacy elsewhere to fill that void. This pursuit is not always about physical attraction; rather, it may be driven by a profound need for understanding, validation, and support. Individuals in extramarital affairs often report that their emotional connections outside of marriage fulfill needs that their primary partners have not addressed, leading to a dangerous cycle of dependency on the affair partner for emotional fulfillment.

Deception plays a crucial role in maintaining the façade of fidelity while engaging in an extramarital affair. The psychological burden of lying can be immense, often leading individuals to compartmentalize their lives. They may create elaborate justifications for their behavior, convincing themselves that their actions are harmless or even justified. This cognitive dissonance can lead to increased anxiety and guilt, but many individuals choose to suppress these feelings to protect their self-image and the relationships they are jeopardizing. Understanding the psychological mechanisms behind these lies can illuminate how individuals navigate the complexities of love, loyalty, and betrayal.

Lastly, the search for identity and self-worth is a common psychological trigger for infidelity. Individuals often engage in affairs as a way to explore aspects of themselves that they feel remain unfulfilled within their primary relationships. This quest for self-discovery can lead to emotional entanglements that serve as a means of validation and affirmation. The affair may represent a rebellion against societal norms or personal expectations, allowing individuals to reconnect with parts of themselves that they feel have been lost. Recognizing this psychological dynamic can help individuals reflect on their motivations for infidelity and the implications it has for their emotional well-being and the health of their primary relationships.

Seeking Validation and Affirmation

In the intricate landscape of extramarital affairs, one psychological underpinning often drives individuals to seek connections outside their primary relationships: the quest for validation and affirmation. This desire is deeply rooted in human psychology, where emotional fulfillment and the need for acknowledgment play pivotal roles in personal identity. For many, the emotional void experienced within a marriage can lead them to seek external relationships that promise the validation they crave. These affairs often serve as a refuge, a space where individuals feel seen, appreciated, and valued—elements that may be perceived as lacking in their primary partnerships.

The pursuit of validation can manifest in various ways. Individuals may engage in extramarital affairs as a means to bolster their self-esteem or to reclaim a sense of lost identity. In a committed relationship, personal needs can sometimes become overshadowed by shared responsibilities, routines, and the demands of daily life. Consequently, individuals may find themselves yearning for acknowledgment, leading them to seek emotional connections that provide immediate gratification and reassurance. This shift highlights a critical psychological aspect of cheating: the search for affirmation can become a driving force that blinds individuals to the potential consequences of their actions.

Emotional affairs, in particular, are often marked by a profound sense of connection and understanding that may be missing in the primary relationship. This dynamic can create a powerful illusion of intimacy, where individuals feel that their thoughts, feelings, and desires are not only heard but celebrated. Such relationships can reinforce a person's self-worth, offering a stark contrast to feelings of neglect or emotional distance experienced within their marriage. However, this validation is often built on fragile foundations, rooted in secrecy and deception, which can ultimately lead to further emotional turmoil when the reality of the affair comes to light.

The psychology behind seeking validation is also intertwined with societal expectations and personal insecurities. Many individuals may feel compelled to conform to certain ideals of success and happiness, which can lead to feelings of inadequacy when their own lives do not align with these standards. In seeking affirmation through extramarital relationships, they may believe they are compensating for perceived shortcomings. This need for external validation can perpetuate a cycle of deceit, where individuals justify their actions as necessary for their emotional survival, rationalizing that the happiness derived from these connections outweighs the guilt of betrayal.

Ultimately, understanding the psychological motivations behind seeking validation and affirmation in extramarital affairs is crucial for those involved in such relationships. It sheds light on the complexities of human emotions and the often tumultuous journey of seeking fulfillment outside established commitments. Acknowledging these motivations is not only essential for fostering personal growth but also for navigating the intricate web of relationships built on secrecy and lies. By recognizing the underlying psychological factors, individuals may find pathways to address their emotional needs constructively, paving the way for healthier connections and a deeper understanding of their own desires and values.

The Role of Unmet Needs in Marriage

Unmet needs in marriage often serve as a catalyst for extramarital affairs, highlighting the complexities of emotional intimacy and personal fulfillment. Within the confines of a committed relationship, individuals may find that their needs for affection, understanding, and companionship are not being met. This lack of fulfillment can lead to feelings of isolation and frustration, prompting some to seek connection outside their marriage. Understanding the psychological underpinnings of these unmet needs is crucial for examining the motivations behind infidelity and the emotional turmoil that often accompanies it.

At the heart of many extramarital affairs lies a longing for emotional connection that is perceived to be lacking in the primary relationship. Individuals may feel that their spouses are unable or unwilling to engage in meaningful conversations or to provide the emotional support they crave. This gap can create a sense of loneliness that drives them to seek validation and intimacy elsewhere. Emotional affairs, in particular, thrive on this dynamic. They often begin as innocent friendships but can quickly escalate as individuals find solace in each other's understanding, inadvertently filling the void left by their partners.

The psychology of cheating reveals that unmet needs are not merely a reflection of personal inadequacies but often stem from broader relational issues. Communication breakdowns, differing expectations, and emotional disconnects within the marriage can contribute to feelings of dissatisfaction. Individuals may rationalize their actions by convincing themselves that their needs are legitimate and that their partners are at fault for not meeting them. This cognitive distortion can further entrench the deception, as individuals engage in extramarital relationships while maintaining the facade of a happy marriage, often leading to a web of lies that complicates their emotional landscape.

Moreover, the role of deception in maintaining an extramarital relationship cannot be understated. As individuals navigate their dual lives, they often resort to elaborate justifications for their infidelity. This deception serves as a protective mechanism, shielding them from the guilt of their actions and providing a temporary escape from the emotional pain of unmet needs. However, this duplicity can also exacerbate feelings of guilt, anxiety, and shame. The emotional toll of living a lie can create an internal conflict that complicates both the affair and the original marriage, often leaving individuals questioning their choices and the authenticity of their connections.

In conclusion, the interplay between unmet needs and extramarital affairs underscores the importance of open communication and emotional vulnerability within marriage. Couples who acknowledge and address their unmet needs stand a better chance of fostering intimacy and connection, potentially reducing the risk of infidelity. By exploring the psychological aspects of emotional affairs and the motivations behind cheating, individuals can gain insights into their behavior and the relational dynamics at play. Ultimately, understanding these factors can pave the way for healthier relationships, whether within the marriage or in the pursuit of more fulfilling connections outside it.

The Secret Lives of Cheaters

Double Lives: Juggling Two Relationships

In the intricate landscape of human relationships, the phenomenon of double lives—particularly in the context of extramarital affairs—reveals a complex interplay of emotions, motivations, and psychological underpinnings. Individuals who engage in multiple romantic partnerships often find themselves navigating a delicate balance, striving to meet the needs of both relationships while simultaneously managing the inherent risks of deception. This subchapter explores how individuals juggle these dual commitments, examining the emotional and psychological implications that arise from leading a double life.

The emotional affair, often characterized by deep connections formed outside of marriage, provides a compelling lens through which to understand this dual existence. Unlike purely physical relationships, emotional affairs thrive on intimacy, vulnerability, and shared experiences that may be lacking in the primary partnership. Individuals may seek these connections to fulfill unmet emotional needs, such as affection, understanding, or even validation. As these relationships develop, they can create a profound sense of fulfillment, but they also introduce significant psychological tension, as individuals grapple with feelings of guilt, anxiety, and the fear of discovery.

The motivations behind extramarital affairs are multifaceted and often deeply rooted in individual psychology. Factors such as dissatisfaction in the primary relationship, a desire for novelty, or even a quest for identity can drive individuals to seek connections outside their marriage. In some cases, an affair may serve as an escape from reality, offering a temporary reprieve from the challenges of daily life. However, this pursuit of emotional or physical fulfillment can lead to a cycle of deception, wherein individuals construct elaborate narratives to maintain the facade of normalcy in both relationships. Understanding these motivations is crucial for those entangled in such affairs, as it sheds light on the underlying emotional currents that propel them into this precarious situation.

Deception plays a central role in the existence of double lives, often manifesting in the form of lies, half-truths, and strategic omissions. Individuals may go to great lengths to conceal their extramarital relationships, crafting detailed cover stories that allow them to maintain their commitments without arousing suspicion. This deception not only creates a web of lies but also fosters a sense of isolation, as the individual grapples with the burden of secrecy. The psychological toll of living a double life can lead to increased anxiety and stress, as the constant fear of exposure looms over both relationships. Navigating this landscape requires a delicate balance of emotional intelligence, self-awareness, and often a significant amount of cognitive dissonance.

Ultimately, the act of juggling two relationships raises profound questions about loyalty, love, and personal authenticity. Individuals in extramarital affairs must confront the ethical implications of their choices and the impact on their partners. While some may rationalize their actions as a means of self-exploration or personal fulfillment, it is essential to recognize the potential for emotional harm to all parties involved. Engaging in open and honest communication with oneself and one's partners may provide a pathway toward greater understanding, healing, and, in some cases, resolution. In the end, the journey through the complexities of double lives serves as a poignant reminder of the intricate nature of human relationships and the profound impact that secrets and lies can have on our emotional well-being.

The Psychology of Secrecy

The act of secrecy is deeply woven into the fabric of human relationships, particularly in the context of extramarital affairs. For individuals engaged in emotional or physical infidelity, secrecy serves not only as a protective mechanism but also as a psychological labyrinth that complicates their emotional landscape. Understanding the psychology of secrecy is crucial for those involved in extramarital affairs, as it sheds light on the motivations behind these relationships and the emotional states they engender. Secrecy can create a false sense of intimacy, allowing individuals to forge connections that feel safe from the scrutiny of their primary relationships.

At the heart of secrecy lies the desire for protection—protection from judgment, rejection, and the potential fallout of revealing one's actions. Many individuals in extramarital affairs experience an internal conflict between their longing for connection with a new partner and their commitment to their spouse. This conflict can lead to a complex web of lies and deceit, where the emotional thrill of a secret relationship becomes intertwined with guilt and anxiety. The psychological burden of maintaining this dual life can be significant, creating an ever-present tension that influences the emotional well-being of those involved. The fear of exposure often leads to an ambivalence about the affair itself, where individuals may simultaneously cherish the emotional escape it provides while grappling with the moral implications of their actions.

The emotional affairs specifically highlight how secrecy can foster a unique psychological dynamic. When partners engage in emotional infidelity, the secrecy surrounding their connection often intensifies the bond they share. This clandestine relationship creates an environment where individuals feel seen, understood, and validated in ways that may be lacking in their primary relationships. However, this emotional intimacy is often built on a foundation of lies, leading to a distorted perception of love and connection. The secrecy becomes a double-edged sword; while it may enhance feelings of closeness with the affair partner, it also cultivates a sense of isolation and disconnection from the spouse, further complicating the emotional landscape.

In addition to the emotional complexities, the

psychology of secrecy involves navigating the motivations that drive individuals to engage in extramarital affairs in the first place. Common motivations include a desire for validation, a quest for excitement, or an attempt to escape from dissatisfaction in the marriage. Understanding these underlying motivations is essential in unpacking the rationale behind the secrecy. Individuals may convince themselves that the affair is justified as a means of fulfilling unmet emotional needs, yet they often fail to recognize the long-term consequences of their choices. This dissonance between justification and reality can lead to a cycle of secrecy that becomes increasingly difficult to break.

Ultimately, the psychology of secrecy in extramarital affairs reveals a complex interplay of emotional needs, motivations, and consequences. For those involved, recognizing the profound impact of secrecy on their emotional state and relationships can be a pivotal step toward personal reflection and growth. Acknowledging the role of deception not only in maintaining the affair but also in shaping one's identity can provide valuable insights. It encourages individuals to confront the realities of their choices, fostering a deeper understanding of themselves and the dynamics at play in their relationships. Through this exploration, individuals may find pathways to navigate their emotional needs more authentically, potentially leading to healthier relationships in the future, whether within or outside the confines of marriage.

Impact on Personal Identity and Self-Perception

Engaging in an extramarital affair can profoundly impact an individual's personal identity and self-perception. For many, the act of infidelity sparks a duality that can lead to an internal conflict between the roles they play in their lives—such as a devoted spouse and a passionate partner. This tension can create a fragmented sense of self, where individuals find it increasingly challenging to reconcile their actions with their values, beliefs, and self-image. As they navigate these conflicting identities, they may start to question who they truly are, leading to a crisis of self-understanding that complicates their emotional landscape.

The emotional connection often experienced in extramarital affairs can add another layer to this complexity. Many individuals enter these relationships seeking fulfillment that may be lacking in their marriages, which can lead to a profound sense of identity reformation. They may perceive themselves as more desirable, vibrant, or alive in the context of the affair, as they experience affection and attention from someone outside their primary relationship. This newfound self-perception can be intoxicating, fostering a sense of empowerment and validation that contrasts sharply with their marital experience. However, this shift can also provoke feelings of guilt and shame, particularly when the reality of their deception becomes difficult to ignore.

The psychology of cheating also plays a crucial role in shaping self-perception. For some, the motivations for pursuing an affair may stem from deeper psychological needs, such as a desire for validation, excitement, or an escape from routine. These motivations can alter how individuals view themselves, as they may start to see themselves as risk-takers or rebels. While this newfound identity may initially feel liberating, it can also cultivate an unhealthy reliance on external validation, which can exacerbate feelings of insecurity and self-doubt once the affair is uncovered or comes to an end.

Maintaining an extramarital relationship often necessitates a web of secrets and lies, which can further distort an individual's self-perception. The effort to uphold this facade can lead individuals to create a persona that is detached from their true selves. They may adopt behaviors and attitudes that align with the expectations of their affair partner, often at the expense of authenticity. As they invest in these deceptive practices, they may develop a distorted self-image, where their sense of self becomes defined more by their ability to deceive than by their genuine qualities and values. This disconnection can result in a profound sense of alienation, both from their partner and from themselves.

Ultimately, the impact of extramarital affairs on personal identity and self-perception is multifaceted. As individuals grapple with the consequences of their actions, they may find themselves at a crossroads, prompting a reevaluation of their life choices, values, and relationships. The journey through this complexity can be painful, yet it also presents an opportunity for deep introspection and growth. By confronting the dissonance between their actions and their self-image, individuals may ultimately emerge with a clearer understanding of themselves and a renewed commitment to authenticity, whether that leads to reconciliation with their spouse or a fresh start on their own terms.

The Role of Deception in Emotional Affairs

Justifying Lies to Maintain Connections

In the complex landscape of human relationships, the act of deception serves various functions, particularly in the context of extramarital affairs. For many involved in these clandestine connections, lies become a necessary tool to navigate the tricky waters of emotional entanglement and secrecy. This subchapter explores the justifications behind these lies, highlighting how individuals rationalize their deceptive behaviors to maintain the fragile connections that exist outside their primary relationships.

One of the primary motivations for lying in the

context of emotional affairs is the desire to protect one's emotional investment. Individuals often find themselves deeply intertwined with their extramarital partners, cultivating bonds that can be as intense as those in their primary relationships. To sustain this emotional connection, they may resort to deception, believing that honesty would jeopardize not only their affair but also their overall emotional well-being. This perspective suggests that the lies serve a protective function, allowing individuals to shield themselves and their partners from uncomfortable truths that could disrupt the delicate balance they have created.

Moreover, the fear of abandonment plays a significant role in the justification of lies. Many individuals engaged in extramarital affairs grapple with insecurities regarding their self-worth and the stability of their primary relationship. The thought of losing the emotional support and validation they derive from their affair can lead them to fabricate stories or mislead their partners. In their minds, these lies are not mere deceptions but rather necessary measures to ensure that their emotional needs are met. This mindset highlights a paradox: the very act of lying, which can erode trust, is perceived as essential for preserving the feelings of connection and intimacy.

Additionally, individuals may justify their lies by focusing on the perceived shortcomings of their primary relationships. When they feel neglected, unappreciated, or emotionally disconnected from their spouses, they may convince themselves that their extramarital affairs are a legitimate response to these deficiencies. In this context, the lies they tell are seen as a way to gain agency over their emotional lives, allowing them to seek fulfillment outside the constraints of their marriages. This rationalization can create a distorted view of fidelity, where emotional affairs are framed as not only acceptable but necessary for personal happiness and satisfaction.

However, the psychological toll of maintaining these lies can be profound. While individuals may initially find comfort in their deceptions, the continuous need to fabricate stories can lead to feelings of guilt, anxiety, and isolation. This internal conflict can create a cycle of emotional distress, where the very lies intended to protect relationships end up causing significant harm. As they navigate this intricate web of secrets, individuals may experience a diminishing sense of authenticity, recognizing that their connections are built on a foundation of untruths rather than genuine understanding and trust.

In conclusion, the justifications for lying in the context of extramarital affairs are deeply rooted in the complexities of human emotion and relational dynamics. These deceptions often arise from a desire to protect emotional investments, a fear of abandonment, and a response to perceived inadequacies in primary relationships. While individuals may believe that their lies are necessary to maintain connections, the psychological ramifications can be significant, often leading to a cycle of guilt and disconnection. Understanding these dynamics is crucial for anyone navigating the treacherous waters of extramarital relationships, as it sheds light on the intricate interplay between love, deception, and the human need for connection.

The Emotional Toll of Sustaining a Deceptive Relationship

The emotional toll of sustaining a deceptive relationship is a complex and multifaceted phenomenon that can deeply affect those involved in extramarital affairs. People engaged in such relationships often grapple with feelings of guilt, anxiety, and internal conflict. These emotions arise not only from the act of deception itself but also from the inherent dissonance between their public personas and private realities. The psychological strain of living a double life can lead to a significant emotional burden, manifesting in stress, depression, and a pervasive sense of unease.

One of the primary emotional consequences of maintaining an extramarital affair is the persistent anxiety that accompanies secrecy. Individuals often find themselves in a state of hyper-vigilance, continually monitoring their words and actions to avoid discovery. This constant fear can be exhausting and lead to heightened levels of stress, which may affect both mental and physical health. The emotional toll is compounded by the necessity of creating elaborate narratives to justify the affair, leaving individuals feeling trapped in a web of deception that is difficult to escape.

Moreover, the emotional connections formed outside of marriage can complicate feelings of loyalty and attachment. Those engaged in emotional affairs may develop deep bonds with their partners, leading to conflicting feelings about their primary relationships. This emotional entanglement can create a sense of isolation, as individuals often feel unable to share the complexities of their situation with friends or family. The resulting emotional turmoil can lead to a cycle of seeking validation and intimacy outside of the marriage while simultaneously feeling guilty about the pain caused to their spouse.

Additionally, the act of deception can erode self-esteem and self-worth. Individuals may struggle with feelings of inadequacy and shame, questioning their decisions and the motivations behind their actions. The cognitive dissonance of wanting to be a loving partner while engaging in betrayal can lead to an identity crisis. This internal struggle may result in a diminished sense of self, where individuals feel defined by their secrets rather than their genuine qualities and values.

Ultimately, the emotional toll of sustaining a deceptive relationship can have long-lasting implications. The psychological effects may extend beyond the affair itself, influencing future relationships and emotional health. Understanding the depths of this emotional burden can empower individuals to confront their realities, seek healing, and, if necessary, reevaluate their priorities in both love and life. Identifying and addressing the emotional consequences of deception is a crucial step toward breaking free from the cycle of infidelity and fostering healthier, more honest connections.

Navigating Guilt and Shame

Navigating guilt and shame is a complex yet essential aspect for individuals involved in extramarital affairs. These emotions often serve as significant barriers to personal clarity and emotional growth. Guilt typically arises from the awareness that one's actions contradict their values or commitments, while shame encompasses a deeper sense of unworthiness or failure. Together, they create a tumultuous emotional landscape that can complicate both the extramarital relationship and the primary marriage. Understanding the roots and implications of these feelings is crucial for anyone engaged in an affair, as they can inform future choices and relationships.

Guilt often manifests in the form of self-reproach, particularly when individuals reflect on the impact of their infidelity on their spouse and family. This feeling can lead to a heightened sense of anxiety and stress, as one grapples with the consequences of their actions. In many cases, guilt acts as a catalyst for change; it compels individuals to reassess their motivations and the emotional needs that led them to seek connections outside their marriage. Acknowledging guilt can promote self-awareness, allowing individuals to confront the underlying issues that their extramarital affair may have masked. It is vital to recognize that feeling guilty does not inherently signify a moral failing but can instead serve as an important signal for personal growth and healing.

Shame, on the other hand, often runs deeper than guilt and can lead to a pervasive sense of inadequacy. Those involved in extramarital affairs may internalize their actions, believing they are fundamentally flawed for their choices. This can create a vicious cycle where shame leads to further deceit as individuals attempt to hide their feelings and actions from themselves and others. It is essential to differentiate between healthy shame, which can motivate positive change, and toxic shame, which can paralyze and inhibit personal development. Understanding this distinction can help individuals navigate their emotions more effectively and foster a healthier self-image.

The interplay of guilt and shame can also complicate the dynamics of the extramarital relationship itself. Partners in an affair may experience a push-pull dynamic where moments of intimacy are tainted by guilt, leading to emotional withdrawal or defensiveness. This can create an environment rife with tension and misunderstandings. Open communication about these feelings can be a powerful tool for both partners to address their emotional needs and establish boundaries. By fostering a safe space for dialogue, individuals can begin to unravel the complexities of their emotions, ultimately leading to a more honest and fulfilling connection—whether that relationship continues or not.

Ultimately, navigating guilt and shame requires a commitment to self-reflection and honesty. Individuals must confront their motivations and the emotional voids that their affairs sought to fill. This process often involves seeking professional guidance, whether through therapy or support groups, to explore these feelings in a constructive manner. By addressing guilt and shame directly, individuals can not only improve their understanding of their current relationship but also pave the way for healthier future connections. In doing so, they may find that the journey through guilt and shame can lead to a deeper understanding of themselves, their desires, and what they truly seek in love and relationships.

Communication Patterns in Extramarital Affairs

How Communication Differs from Monogamous Relationships

In the realm of relationships, communication serves as the bedrock of connection, yet its nature and function can vary significantly between monogamous partnerships and those characterized by extramarital affairs. In monogamous relationships, communication typically aims to foster intimacy, trust, and long-term commitment. Partners engage in dialogues that reinforce their emotional bonds, address conflicts, and navigate shared responsibilities. Conversely, in extramarital affairs, the communication often takes on a different tone, primarily focused on secrecy and the cultivation of a clandestine emotional connection. This divergence in communication styles reflects the unique psychological dynamics at play in these relationships, where the thrill of the forbidden can overshadow the need for open dialogue.

One of the most notable differences in communication within extramarital affairs is the presence of deception. Partners in monogamous relationships generally strive for transparency as a means of building trust and mutual understanding. However, in extramarital situations, deception becomes a fundamental component. Individuals may engage in extensive fabrications to conceal their actions from their spouses, leading to a communication style heavily laden with lies, half-truths, and omissions. This environment not only complicates the relationship dynamics but also creates a psychological burden, as partners continuously navigate the tension between their desires and the need to maintain the facade of normalcy in their primary relationships.

In emotional affairs, the communication often shifts from a shared dialogue about a life together to a more insular form of interaction that focuses on personal needs and desires. Participants may find solace in the emotional connection they share, leading to discussions that are deeply personal and revealing. This aspect can foster a sense of intimacy that is often absent in their primary relationships. However, this intensity can be misleading; while it may feel genuine, it is often built upon a foundation of secrecy and betrayal. The emotional highs that accompany these connections can obscure the reality of the situation, creating a dissonance between how partners perceive their connection and the underlying deceit that sustains it.

Moreover, the motivations behind communication in extramarital affairs differ significantly from those in monogamous relationships. In a committed partnership, discussions often revolve around future aspirations, mutual support, and conflict resolution. In contrast, communication in affairs may be driven by immediate gratification and the escape from the perceived constraints of monogamy. This can lead to a superficial exchange of sentiments, where the focus is predominantly on the thrill of the moment rather than on building a lasting emotional framework. As a result, individuals engaging in these affairs may find themselves trapped in a cycle of fleeting connections, where the depth of communication is sacrificed for the excitement of the liaison.

Ultimately, the differences in communication patterns between monogamous relationships and extramarital affairs highlight the psychological complexities that underpin these experiences. The reliance on deception, the focus on personal gratification, and the often superficial nature of exchanges in extramarital encounters can create an illusory sense of intimacy. This chapter seeks to illuminate these distinctions, offering a deeper understanding of how communication operates in the shadows of love, where secrets and lies can overshadow genuine connection. By recognizing these patterns, individuals may gain insights into their motivations and the emotional toll of maintaining relationships built on deception, fostering a path toward greater self-awareness and, potentially, healthier relational choices.

The Use of Technology and Secrecy

In the contemporary landscape of relationships, technology has transformed the way individuals communicate, connect, and, regrettably, deceive. For those engaged in extramarital affairs, the digital world presents both opportunities and risks. The use of smartphones, social media, and various messaging applications has created an environment where maintaining secrecy can be both easier and more complex. Understanding the role of technology in these hidden relationships is crucial for navigating the emotional and psychological ramifications that accompany such choices.

One of the primary advantages technology

offers to individuals in extramarital affairs is the ability to communicate discreetly. Encrypted messaging apps and private social media accounts can facilitate intimate conversations without the risk of detection. This anonymity can foster a sense of safety, allowing individuals to express their feelings and desires without the fear of their spouse discovering their indiscretions. However, this reliance on technology also introduces a layer of psychological complexity. The very tools that enable secrecy can create a sense of paranoia, as individuals may obsessively check for signs of exposure or feel anxious about their partner's potential access to their digital communications.

Moreover, technology serves as a double-edged sword in emotional affairs. While it can enhance the emotional connection between partners outside of marriage through constant communication, it can also lead to feelings of guilt and anxiety. The ease of sharing personal thoughts and experiences can deepen emotional bonds, yet the underlying deception can create an internal conflict. Individuals may find themselves torn between the thrill of their emotional connection and the moral implications of their actions. This psychological tension can lead to a cycle of secrecy and lies that is difficult to break, often exacerbated by the very technology that facilitates the affair.

The psychology of cheating is further complicated by the role of social media. Platforms like Facebook and Instagram not only provide opportunities for clandestine interactions but also serve as a space for projection and idealization of relationships. Individuals may curate their online personas to showcase a life filled with excitement and passion, contrasting sharply with their mundane marital realities. This disconnect can fuel desires for emotional affairs as individuals seek validation and fulfillment that they feel is lacking in their primary relationships. The juxtaposition of public perception and private reality can create a fertile ground for deception, as individuals craft narratives that serve their needs while neglecting the truth.

Ultimately, the intersection of technology and secrecy in extramarital affairs highlights the intricate psychological dynamics at play. While technology can facilitate connections that provide emotional sustenance, it also perpetuates a cycle of deceit that can have profound effects on individuals and their relationships. Understanding these dynamics is essential for those involved in emotional affairs, as it allows for a deeper exploration of their motivations and the consequences of their actions. Engaging with these complexities can lead to greater self-awareness and, potentially, healthier relational choices, whether that involves addressing the underlying issues within their marriages or reevaluating the paths they choose to pursue.

Emotional Manipulation and Control

Emotional manipulation and control are critical elements that often underpin extramarital affairs, shaping the dynamics between partners involved in these clandestine relationships. Individuals may engage in emotional manipulation to gain a sense of power or to fulfill unmet needs that they perceive are lacking in their primary relationships. This manipulation can take many forms, from subtle gaslighting to overt emotional blackmail, and is frequently employed to maintain secrecy and prevent the dissolution of both the affair and the primary relationship. Understanding these patterns can provide clarity for individuals caught in the web of emotional affairs, enabling them to recognize unhealthy dynamics and make informed decisions about their emotional well-being.

In the context of emotional affairs, the psychological aspects of manipulation often manifest through the creation of an idealized version of the affair partner. This idealization can lead to an emotional dependency that creates a false sense of fulfillment, making it difficult for individuals to confront the realities of their primary relationships. Manipulators may use flattery, affection, and attention to cultivate a deep emotional bond, thereby reinforcing the affair's significance in the individual's life. This bond can be intoxicating, blurring the lines between genuine connection and emotional control. It's essential for those involved in such affairs to critically evaluate their feelings and the motivations behind the emotional exchanges that occur, fostering greater awareness of their own vulnerabilities.

The psychology behind cheating reveals that many individuals engage in extramarital affairs as a response to unmet emotional needs. Loneliness, lack of intimacy, and unmet desires can drive partners to seek solace outside their marriages. Emotional manipulators exploit these vulnerabilities, often promising the emotional fulfillment that their victims crave. This dynamic not only perpetuates the affair but also deepens the emotional entanglement, as individuals become increasingly reliant on the manipulated emotions to fill the void left by their primary relationships. Consequently, this reliance can lead to a cycle of deceit, where individuals justify their actions to themselves and others, believing that the emotional connection is worth the risks involved.

Deception plays a pivotal role in maintaining the facade of both the extramarital relationship and the primary marriage. Emotional manipulators may resort to lying or omitting critical information to keep their partner compliant and invested in the affair. This can create an environment where secrets flourish, leading to a web of lies that ultimately complicates the emotional landscape for everyone involved. The emotional toll of such manipulation can be profound, often resulting in feelings of guilt, shame, and confusion as individuals grapple with conflicting loyalties and desires. Recognizing these manipulative tactics can empower those entangled in emotional affairs to assert their boundaries and seek healthier forms of connection.

Ultimately, understanding emotional manipulation and control within the context of extramarital affairs is crucial for anyone navigating these complex emotional landscapes. By identifying the patterns of manipulation and the motivations behind them, individuals can begin to disentangle their emotional experiences from the deceptive dynamics at play. This awareness can lead to healthier decision-making, whether that means confronting the truth about their primary relationships or reevaluating the emotional connections forged in affairs. As individuals gain insight into the psychological underpinnings of their experiences, they can work toward fostering genuine emotional fulfillment, both within themselves and in their future relationships.

The Consequences of Cheating

Psychological Impact on the Cheater

The psychological impact on individuals engaged in extramarital affairs is a complex interplay of emotions, guilt, and internal conflict. While many may initially seek excitement or validation outside their primary relationship, the reality of cheating often leads to profound psychological consequences that can affect both the cheater and their partner. Understanding these impacts is crucial for those involved in such relationships, as it sheds light on the deeper motivations behind their actions and the emotional turmoil that can ensue.

One of the most significant psychological effects is the pervasive sense of guilt. Cheaters often experience a moral conflict, torn between the excitement of the affair and the loyalty they owe to their spouse or partner. This internal struggle can lead to anxiety, depression, and feelings of worthlessness, as individuals grapple with the disparity between their actions and their values. The thrill that initially accompanies the affair may be overshadowed by a lingering sense of shame, forcing the individual to confront their choices and the potential fallout from their deception.

Moreover, many cheaters report feelings of isolation and loneliness, exacerbated by the need to maintain secrecy. The clandestine nature of extramarital affairs often means that those involved cannot share their experiences or seek support from friends and family. This secrecy can lead to a heightened sense of paranoia, as the fear of being discovered creates an environment of constant stress. As a result, the cheater may find themselves emotionally distanced from both their partner and the person with whom they are having the affair, leading to a cycle of emotional disconnect that can be difficult to break.

The psychological ramifications extend beyond immediate feelings of guilt and isolation. Many individuals in extramarital affairs wrestle with questions of self-worth and identity. The affair may serve as a temporary escape from dissatisfaction in their primary relationship, but it can also lead to a crisis of identity as they confront the reasons behind their infidelity. This introspection can be both enlightening and painful, prompting individuals to reassess their values, desires, and the choices they have made. In some cases, this process can lead to personal growth, but it often requires facing uncomfortable truths about oneself and the motivations for seeking emotional connection outside of marriage.

Ultimately, the psychological impact on the cheater is a multifaceted experience that combines excitement with guilt, isolation, and self-reflection. For those involved in extramarital affairs, it is essential to acknowledge these psychological effects and consider the long-term implications of their actions. By understanding the complexities of their emotions, individuals may find an opportunity for growth and, potentially, reconciliation with their partner. Addressing the psychological aspects of cheating is a vital step in navigating the tumultuous waters of infidelity, allowing individuals to make more informed choices about their relationships moving forward.

Effects on the Primary Relationship

The dynamics of an extramarital affair can significantly impact the primary relationship, often leading to profound psychological and emotional consequences. For individuals engaged in emotional affairs, the allure of intimacy and connection outside of marriage can create a complex web of feelings that ultimately influences how partners interact within their primary relationship. This subchapter aims to dissect the multifaceted effects of such affairs on the foundational aspects of a partnership, including trust, communication, and emotional intimacy.

One of the most immediate repercussions of an extramarital affair is the erosion of trust. Trust serves as the cornerstone of any committed relationship, and its breach can lead to feelings of betrayal and insecurity. Partners in a primary relationship may find themselves grappling with doubt and suspicion, questioning not only the fidelity of their spouse but also the authenticity of their shared experiences. This shift can create an atmosphere of defensiveness, making open communication increasingly difficult. As a result, the primary relationship may devolve into a cycle of accusation and denial, further alienating the partners from one another.

Emotional connections forged through infidelity can also distort perceptions of the primary relationship. Individuals may begin to compare their spouse unfavorably with the emotional partner, leading to discontent and resentment. The excitement and novelty of the affair can overshadow the realities of marital life, causing dissatisfaction to fester. This comparison often leads to unrealistic expectations, which can create additional strain as partners strive to fulfill needs that were once met within the bounds of their marriage. Over time, this can contribute to a widening emotional gap, leaving both partners feeling disconnected and unfulfilled.

In addition to trust and emotional comparison, communication patterns are frequently altered in the wake of an affair. The need to maintain secrecy can lead to a breakdown in honest dialogue, as the individual involved in the affair may become adept at crafting lies or withholding information. This behavior can lead to a communication vacuum where genuine discussions about feelings, needs, and desires are replaced by superficial interactions. As partners become more guarded, the emotional distance can deepen, making it increasingly challenging to address underlying issues or rekindle the intimacy that once characterized their relationship.

Ultimately, the effects of an extramarital affair on the primary relationship can be profound and far-reaching. While some couples may find a pathway to reconciliation, many face the daunting task of rebuilding what has been lost. This process often requires confronting the reality of the affair, understanding its motivations, and navigating the complexities of forgiveness. Partners may need to engage in difficult conversations about their needs and expectations, as well as the values that underpin their commitment to one another. In doing so, they can begin to rebuild trust and foster a healthier emotional connection, transforming their relationship into a more resilient partnership.

Long-term Ramifications of Infidelity

Infidelity, whether emotional or physical, often carries consequences that extend far beyond the immediate thrill of secrecy or the fleeting excitement of an affair. Those involved in extramarital relationships frequently overlook the profound psychological and emotional ramifications that can ensue. The initial allure may feel intoxicating, but the long-term effects can lead to significant emotional distress, relationship deterioration, and a pervasive sense of guilt that lingers long after the affair has ended. Understanding these ramifications is crucial for anyone navigating the complexities of infidelity.

One immediate consequence of engaging in an extramarital affair is the emotional turmoil that follows the deception. Individuals may experience heightened anxiety, guilt, and fear of discovery, which can erode their mental health over time. This internal conflict can lead to a pervasive sense of instability, affecting not only the individual but also the dynamics within their primary relationship. As trust erodes, partners may find themselves ensnared in a cycle of suspicion and resentment, ultimately diminishing the emotional intimacy that once formed the bedrock of their bond.

In addition to personal emotional struggles, the ramifications of infidelity can extend to the broader social context. Relationships with friends and family may be strained as the affair forces individuals to maintain a web of lies, further isolating them from their support systems. This secrecy can create an environment where individuals feel increasingly alienated, as they grapple with the duality of their lives. The emotional connections fostered during an affair often lack the depth and stability found in more authentic relationships, leading to a sense of emptiness and disconnection that persists even after the affair has ended.

Another significant long-term effect of infidelity is the potential for trauma within the primary relationship. Betrayal can lead to profound emotional scars for both partners, often resulting in long-lasting damage that transcends the affair itself. Trust, once broken, can be exceedingly difficult to rebuild, leaving lasting imprints of insecurity and doubt. Partners may find themselves constantly questioning each other's loyalty, leading to a cycle of jealousy and insecurity that can suffocate the relationship. This trauma can perpetuate a negative cycle, where unresolved issues from the affair continue to affect the couple's interactions long after the event.

Finally, the motivations behind the affair play a critical role in determining the long-term ramifications of infidelity. Individuals who engage in emotional affairs often do so in search of validation, excitement, or an escape from dissatisfaction in their primary relationship. If these underlying issues remain unaddressed, the individual may find themselves repeating the cycle of infidelity, leading to a pattern of destructive behavior that complicates their emotional landscape. Recognizing and addressing the root causes of infidelity is essential for fostering healing and breaking free from the patterns of deception. Ultimately, acknowledging the long-term ramifications of infidelity can empower individuals to make more informed choices about their relationships and emotional well-being.

Ending the Cycle of Deception

Recognizing Patterns of Behavior

Recognizing patterns of behavior is crucial for anyone navigating the complex emotional landscape of extramarital affairs. In these situations, individuals often find themselves caught between conflicting desires, leading to behaviors that can sometimes be subconscious. Understanding these patterns is not just about self-awareness; it is also about comprehending the psychological mechanisms that drive individuals to seek emotional connections outside their primary relationships. By identifying these behaviors, individuals can gain insight into their motivations and the dynamics at play in their relationships.

One of the most common patterns observed in emotional affairs is the gradual shift in emotional investment. Initially, the affair may begin as a fleeting attraction or a simple friendship, but over time, it can develop into a profound emotional connection. This transformation often reflects unmet needs in the primary relationship, such as intimacy, validation, or understanding. Recognizing this pattern can help individuals reflect on what is missing in their marriage and whether these needs can be addressed within that context, rather than through deceitful means.

Another significant behavior pattern is the tendency to compartmentalize relationships. Those involved in extramarital affairs often create distinct boundaries between their primary and secondary partners. This compartmentalization allows individuals to maintain a facade of normalcy in their marriage while simultaneously nurturing an intense emotional bond outside of it. However, this behavior can lead to increased cognitive dissonance, as individuals struggle to reconcile their actions with their self-image and values. Acknowledging this pattern can prompt deeper introspection about the consequences of such compartmentalization, both for oneself and for those involved.

Deception plays a pivotal role in the dynamics of extramarital affairs, influencing behaviors and emotional responses. Individuals may develop elaborate strategies to conceal their activities, leading to a cycle of lies that can become increasingly complex. Common behaviors include avoiding certain topics, creating alibis, and exhibiting defensive postures when questioned about their whereabouts. Recognizing these deceptive patterns is essential for individuals to understand how their actions not only affect their primary partner but also perpetuate a cycle of dishonesty that can be psychologically damaging in the long run.

Finally, recognizing patterns of behavior in extramarital affairs can serve as a catalyst for change. Once individuals become aware of the underlying motivations and emotional triggers driving their actions, they can begin to make more informed choices about their relationships. This awareness can lead to healthier communication with their primary partners, a reevaluation of their emotional needs, and ultimately, the possibility of healing and growth. Whether one chooses to remain in the affair or address the issues within the marriage, understanding these behavioral patterns is a vital step toward reclaiming agency and fostering authentic connections.

Strategies for Healing and Moving Forward

In navigating the complex emotional landscape of extramarital affairs, it becomes essential to develop strategies for healing and moving forward. The emotional toll of betrayal—whether experienced as the betrayer or the betrayed—can be profound, often leading to feelings of guilt, shame, and confusion. Understanding that healing is a process rather than a destination is crucial. This journey requires a commitment to self-reflection, open communication, and the willingness to confront uncomfortable truths about oneself and one's relationships.

One of the first steps toward healing is to engage in honest self-assessment. Individuals involved in emotional affairs should examine their motivations and the underlying needs that led them to seek connections outside their primary relationship. This exploration can reveal unmet emotional needs, personal insecurities, or dissatisfaction within the marriage. By acknowledging these factors, one can begin to understand the patterns of behavior that contributed to the affair. This self-awareness is fundamental, as it lays the groundwork for making informed choices moving forward, whether that means working to repair the primary relationship or understanding the need for a new direction in life.

Open and honest communication is another vital strategy in the healing process. For couples affected by an extramarital affair, discussing the situation candidly can be both daunting and necessary. It is important to create a safe space where both partners can express their feelings without fear of judgment or retaliation. This dialogue should focus on understanding the emotional gaps that led to the affair, as well as addressing feelings of betrayal and hurt. Effective communication fosters empathy and can help rebuild trust, which is often shattered in the wake of infidelity. Engaging in couples therapy may also provide a supportive environment for these discussions, offering professional guidance to navigate the complexities of emotions involved.

Forgiveness—both of oneself and the partner—plays a crucial role in the healing journey. Forgiveness does not imply condoning the behavior but rather liberating oneself from the burden of resentment and anger. It requires a conscious decision to let go of the past and the associated pain. This process can be gradual and may involve revisiting the incident multiple times, allowing individuals to process their emotions fully. By practicing forgiveness, individuals can pave the way for personal healing and, if desired, for the restoration of their relationship. It is essential to remember that forgiveness is more about personal peace than reconciliation; it is a gift one gives to oneself to foster emotional well-being.

Lastly, moving forward necessitates setting

new intentions for the future. This involves not only addressing the immediate aftermath of the affair but also redefining personal values and relationship goals. Individuals should consider what they truly want from their relationships and how they can align their actions with those desires. This may include fostering healthier emotional connections, prioritizing transparency and trust, and establishing boundaries that prevent future infidelity. Whether one chooses to remain in the marriage or pursue new paths, embracing a proactive approach to relationships can transform the lessons learned from the affair into a foundation for emotional growth and healthier interactions.

In conclusion, healing from extramarital affairs is a multifaceted process that demands introspection, communication, forgiveness, and intentionality. By employing these strategies, individuals can navigate the emotional aftermath of their choices, ultimately leading to a deeper understanding of themselves and their relational dynamics. Acknowledging the complexity of human emotions and the reasons behind deception can empower individuals to make choices that foster healthier, more fulfilling emotional connections, whether within or outside the confines of marriage.

Building Healthy Relationships Post-Affair

Building healthy relationships post-affair is a critical yet challenging endeavor for individuals navigating the aftermath of infidelity. Whether the affair was emotional, physical, or a combination of both, the journey towards rebuilding trust and connection requires introspection, communication, and a commitment to change. Understanding the psychological underpinnings of why the affair occurred can provide valuable insights into how to move forward. This subchapter aims to guide individuals through the complexities of healing and restoring their primary relationship while acknowledging the emotional turmoil that often accompanies such experiences.

The first step in rebuilding a relationship post-affair is acknowledging the breach of trust that has occurred. Both partners must engage in open and honest dialogue about the affair's nature and the emotions it evoked. This conversation should not only explore the reasons behind the infidelity but also allow both partners to express their feelings of hurt, betrayal, and confusion. This process of emotional transparency is essential for fostering an environment where healing can begin. It is crucial to approach these discussions with empathy, as recognizing the pain caused by the affair is foundational in initiating the path toward reconciliation.

Next, establishing clear boundaries is vital for restoring safety and security within the relationship. This involves redefining what trust means for both partners and agreeing upon the necessary steps to rebuild that trust. For the partner who was unfaithful, demonstrating accountability through consistent actions and open communication is essential. For the betrayed partner, articulating their needs and expectations is equally important. This mutual agreement on boundaries serves as a framework through which both individuals can navigate their feelings and behaviors, ultimately creating a more secure emotional landscape.

Additionally, addressing the emotional aspects that led to the affair is crucial for long-term healing. Individuals involved in extramarital relationships often grapple with unmet needs or unresolved issues within their primary partnership. Engaging in individual or couple's therapy can provide a safe space to explore these underlying factors. By examining the motivations for the affair—whether they stem from a desire for validation, excitement, or emotional connection—couples can begin to understand the dynamics that contributed to the infidelity. Such exploration not only aids in personal growth but also helps in redefining the relationship's foundation to prevent future transgressions.

Finally, it is essential to focus on rebuilding intimacy and connection in the aftermath of an affair. This process may involve revisiting shared interests, fostering new experiences together, and actively working on communication skills. Re-establishing emotional and physical intimacy takes time and effort, but it is a vital component of a healthy relationship. Couples should prioritize quality time, engage in affectionate gestures, and create opportunities for vulnerability. By investing in the relationship and nurturing the bond, partners can cultivate a deeper understanding of each other, ultimately leading to a more resilient and fulfilling partnership.

In conclusion, the journey of building healthy relationships post-affair is complex but achievable with dedication and effort. By acknowledging the breach of trust, establishing clear boundaries, addressing emotional undercurrents, and focusing on rebuilding intimacy, couples can navigate the challenges of infidelity. This process not only fosters healing but also paves the way for a more authentic and connected relationship. Embracing this journey requires patience, compassion, and a willingness to grow, transforming a painful experience into an opportunity for deeper understanding and renewed love.

Seeking Help: Therapy and Support

The Role of Therapy in Understanding Infidelity

The exploration of infidelity often leads to a complex web of emotions, motivations, and consequences. Therapy plays a crucial role in helping individuals and couples understand the underlying dynamics that contribute to extramarital affairs. For those engaged in emotional affairs, therapy provides a safe space to unravel the psychological aspects of their actions. Through guided discussions, individuals can confront their feelings, motivations, and the emotional voids they may be attempting to fill outside their primary relationships. This introspection is vital for acknowledging the nuances of their emotional connections, allowing them to gain insight into why they sought solace elsewhere.

In the context of the psychology of cheating, therapy allows individuals to examine the motivations behind their decisions. Cheating is rarely a black-and-white issue; it is often rooted in deeper psychological patterns, such as unmet needs, fear of intimacy, or unresolved past traumas. A skilled therapist can help clients explore these motivations, enabling them to understand their behavior within a broader psychological framework. This understanding is essential not only for personal growth but also for fostering healthier future relationships. By addressing the reasons for their infidelity, individuals can begin to make more conscious choices rather than being driven by impulse or emotional distress.

Deception is another critical aspect of extramarital affairs that therapy can help unravel. Maintaining secrets and lies can create a significant emotional burden, leading to feelings of guilt, shame, and anxiety. Therapy encourages openness and honesty, allowing individuals to confront the consequences of their deception. In this safe environment, clients can explore the fear of being discovered, the guilt associated with lying, and the emotional toll of living a double life. By processing these feelings, individuals can begin to release the weight of their secrets and understand how deception has affected their sense of self and their relationships.

Moreover, therapy offers strategies for rebuilding trust and fostering communication, whether within the context of the primary relationship or in the aftermath of an affair. For those who wish to repair their marriage, understanding the role of infidelity in their relationship dynamics is crucial. Couples therapy can facilitate difficult conversations about expectations, desires, and boundaries, helping both partners articulate their needs more effectively. For those who decide to end their primary relationship, therapy can assist in navigating the emotional fallout and establishing healthier patterns in future relationships. The goal is not only to address the infidelity but also to foster a deeper understanding of oneself and how to engage in healthier relational patterns moving forward.

Ultimately, the role of therapy in understanding infidelity is multifaceted, offering insights into emotional affairs, motivations for cheating, and the complexities of deception. By engaging in therapeutic work, individuals can transform their experiences into opportunities for growth and self-discovery. This journey is not just about addressing the betrayal but also about understanding the self and one's relational needs. As individuals gain clarity and insight through therapy, they can develop a healthier relationship with themselves and others, paving the way for more authentic connections in the future.

Support Groups and Community Resources

Support groups and community resources play a crucial role in the lives of individuals involved in extramarital affairs, particularly when exploring the psychological complexities and emotional ramifications of their choices. These groups provide a safe space for individuals to share their experiences, confront their feelings, and understand the motivations driving their actions. Engaging in open dialogues with others who have faced similar situations can help individuals recognize that they are not alone in their struggles, fostering a sense of community and support in what can often feel like an isolating experience.

The emotional aspect of extramarital affairs is often intertwined with feelings of guilt, shame, and confusion. Support groups can serve as a therapeutic environment where participants can openly express these emotions without fear of judgment. In these settings, individuals are encouraged to reflect on their emotional connections outside of marriage, which can often reveal underlying issues within their primary relationships. Understanding these dynamics can be the first step toward addressing personal needs and desires, ultimately leading to healthier relational patterns, whether that means working on their marriage or choosing to pursue different paths.

In addition to emotional support, community resources can offer educational workshops and seminars that delve into the psychology of cheating. These programs typically explore the various motivations behind extramarital affairs, such as unmet emotional needs, desire for novelty, or escape from dissatisfaction. By understanding these factors, individuals can gain deeper insights into their behaviors and the consequences of their actions. This knowledge can empower them to make informed decisions about their relationships moving forward, whether that involves pursuing therapy, seeking reconciliation, or ending harmful patterns.

Another critical aspect of support groups and community resources is the emphasis on honesty and transparency. Many individuals engaged in extramarital affairs grapple with the burden of secrecy and deception. Participating in a support group can help individuals recognize the detrimental effects of lies—not only on their partners but also on themselves. By fostering an environment that prioritizes honesty, participants can learn to navigate their relationships with greater integrity, ultimately leading to healthier interactions in all areas of their lives.

Ultimately, the journey through the

complexities of extramarital affairs can be tumultuous and fraught with emotional challenges. However, by utilizing support groups and community resources, individuals can find validation, understanding, and tools to address their unique situations. Engaging with others who share similar experiences can lead to profound personal growth and healing, helping individuals to unravel the web of secrets and lies that often accompany their choices, while also guiding them toward a more authentic and fulfilling relational existence.

Creating a Path to Forgiveness and Rebuilding Trust

Creating a path to forgiveness and rebuilding trust is a complex yet essential process for individuals embroiled in extramarital affairs. The emotional turmoil that accompanies infidelity can create a chasm between partners, often leaving feelings of betrayal, anger, and sadness in its wake. Understanding that forgiveness is not merely a gift to the unfaithful partner but a necessary step for the victim to reclaim their emotional well-being is crucial. This journey begins with acknowledging the pain caused by the affair, allowing both partners to express their feelings in a safe environment. Open dialogue about hurt, disappointment, and anger is vital, as it lays the groundwork for healing and understanding.

The first step towards forgiveness involves recognizing the underlying motivations that led to the extramarital involvement. Individuals often engage in emotional affairs to fulfill unmet needs, such as intimacy, validation, or excitement. By exploring these motivations, both partners can gain insight into the dynamics of their relationship. This exploration not only helps the betrayed partner understand the rationale behind the affair but also encourages the unfaithful partner to confront their own insecurities and desires. Acknowledging these feelings can create a foundation for empathy, fostering an environment where healing can begin.

Rebuilding trust is a gradual process that requires consistent effort and commitment from both partners. The unfaithful partner must demonstrate accountability through transparency and honesty. This may involve sharing details about their actions during the affair, as uncomfortable as it may be. Establishing new boundaries and guidelines for the relationship helps create a sense of security for the betrayed partner. Both partners should engage in discussions about their expectations moving forward, ensuring that they are on the same page. Commitment to change is essential; without it, any attempts at rebuilding trust may be perceived as insincere.

As the healing process unfolds, it is important to foster emotional intimacy between partners. This involves engaging in activities that promote connection, such as open discussions about feelings, spending quality time together, and exploring shared interests. Couples may also consider seeking professional help through therapy, where a trained facilitator can guide them through their emotional landscape. This space can provide tools for effective communication, conflict resolution, and understanding, all of which are vital components in restoring trust and intimacy within the relationship.

Finally, forgiveness is an ongoing journey rather than a one-time act. Both partners must recognize that healing from betrayal takes time and that setbacks may occur along the way. Celebrating small victories and milestones in the rebuilding process can help maintain motivation and reinforce the commitment to each other. It is crucial to remember that forgiveness does not mean forgetting the past but rather acknowledging it as a part of the relationship's history. By embracing this journey together, couples can emerge stronger and more resilient, transforming their relationship into one built on renewed trust and deeper emotional connections.

Embracing Authenticity in Love

The Importance of Honesty in Relationships

Honesty is often touted as the cornerstone of any healthy relationship, yet its significance is magnified in the context of extramarital affairs. For those engaged in emotional or physical infidelities, the delicate balance between desire and deception can create a complex web of psychological consequences. Understanding the importance of honesty, even in the shadows of betrayal, can illuminate pathways toward both personal growth and healthier relational dynamics. For individuals involved in extramarital affairs, acknowledging the benefits of honesty can lead to a greater understanding of themselves and their motivations, ultimately fostering a more authentic emotional experience.

In the realm of emotional affairs, where connections are often built on deep psychological bonds, honesty serves as a critical bridge between genuine intimacy and the facade of secrecy. While it may seem counterintuitive to advocate for honesty in a relationship predicated on deception, embracing transparency can help clarify the motivations behind the affair. Individuals often enter these relationships seeking emotional fulfillment that may be lacking in their primary partnerships. By being honest about their feelings, needs, and the reasons for their extramarital involvement, individuals can better navigate their emotional landscapes and make informed decisions about their relationships.

Moreover, the psychology of cheating reveals that many individuals engage in affairs out of a desire to escape from unmet needs within their primary relationship. This yearning, when left unaddressed, can lead to a cycle of dishonesty that only exacerbates feelings of guilt and shame. By fostering a mindset of honesty, individuals can confront the underlying issues that prompted their infidelity in the first place. This not only allows for introspection but also encourages open dialogue with partners, which can either lead to reconciliation or a more constructive separation. The act of being truthful about one's feelings and desires creates opportunities for personal accountability and growth, rather than remaining trapped in a cycle of deception.

Furthermore, the role of deception in

maintaining an extramarital relationship often generates a sense of isolation for those involved. The secrecy can create barriers that prevent individuals from forming authentic connections, both with their affair partner and within their primary relationship. When honesty is introduced, it acts as a catalyst for emotional clarity, allowing individuals to confront their true feelings and the consequences of their actions. This can facilitate a healthier emotional exchange, where both partners can express their needs without the burden of lies. By embracing honesty, individuals can not only enhance their relationships but also alleviate the psychological toll that deception often brings.

Ultimately, the importance of honesty in relationships, particularly in the context of extramarital affairs, cannot be overstated. It serves as a foundation for self-awareness and emotional integrity, allowing individuals to explore their motivations and desires more deeply. While the path of honesty may be fraught with challenges, it holds the potential for healing and transformation. Whether one chooses to remain in their primary partnership or pursue a new direction, the commitment to honesty can lead to more fulfilling and authentic connections. In a landscape often dominated by secrets and lies, choosing to embrace honesty is a powerful step toward reclaiming one's emotional truth.

Moving Beyond Secrets: Cultivating Transparency

In the complex landscape of extramarital affairs, the act of deception often creates an intricate web of secrets and lies that can be difficult to navigate. However, moving beyond these shadows and cultivating transparency can lead to a more authentic understanding of oneself and one's relationships. Transparency is not merely the absence of deceit; it involves an active commitment to honesty, vulnerability, and open communication. By embracing transparency, individuals in extramarital affairs can begin to unravel the motivations and emotions that drive their choices, fostering a healthier approach to their connections outside of marriage.

Understanding the psychological aspects of emotional affairs is crucial for cultivating transparency. Many individuals find themselves drawn into these relationships not solely for physical intimacy but for the emotional fulfillment that may be lacking in their primary partnerships. This emotional connection often thrives on shared secrets and unspoken truths. By acknowledging the underlying feelings that lead to these connections, individuals can begin to express their needs and desires more openly. This shift requires courage and vulnerability, as discussing the emotional voids that drive them to seek validation outside their marriage can be uncomfortable. However, this honesty is essential for fostering a deeper understanding of oneself and the dynamics of the relationship.

The motivations behind cheating are as varied as the individuals involved, ranging from a desire for excitement to feelings of neglect or unfulfillment. To cultivate transparency, it is vital to analyze these motivations critically. Engaging in self-reflection can help individuals recognize patterns in their behavior and emotions that contribute to their decisions. When individuals confront the reasons behind their extramarital affairs with honesty, they can begin to communicate more effectively with their partners, whether that involves seeking change within the marriage or making more informed decisions about their extramarital connections. This level of self-awareness lays the groundwork for a transparent dialogue that can lead to personal growth and healthier relationships.

Transparency also requires a commitment to honesty not only with oneself but also with others involved in the affair. This means establishing clear boundaries and expectations, which can be challenging but ultimately rewarding. Communicating openly about each person's needs, desires, and limitations can help prevent misunderstandings and emotional distress. While the fear of conflict and the potential for hurt feelings may deter individuals from having these conversations, avoiding them can lead to greater deception and emotional turmoil. By fostering an environment where honesty is valued, individuals can build a foundation of trust that enhances the emotional connection within the affair and promotes healthier interactions.

Ultimately, moving beyond secrets and cultivating transparency is about fostering a sense of integrity in one's relationships, whether they are romantic or otherwise. This process involves recognizing the impact of secrecy on emotional well-being and the dynamics of relationships. By prioritizing open communication and vulnerability, individuals can create a space where their true selves can emerge, leading to more fulfilling connections. While the journey toward transparency may be fraught with challenges, the rewards—greater self-awareness, healthier relationships, and emotional fulfillment—are invaluable. Embracing this journey not only enriches personal growth but also paves the way for deeper understanding and connection in all aspects of life.

The Future of Relationships:

Lessons Learned from Deception

The complexities of human relationships have always been a fertile ground for exploration, particularly in the context of extramarital affairs. As we delve into the future of relationships, insights gleaned from experiences of deception provide a framework for understanding the evolving dynamics of love and fidelity. Individuals engaged in emotional affairs often find themselves entangled in a web of secrecy and lies, leading to profound emotional consequences. By examining these lessons, we can better navigate the intricate landscape of human connection and foster healthier relationships moving forward.

One of the most significant lessons learned from deception in extramarital affairs is the importance of open communication. Many individuals involved in emotional affairs often seek validation and intimacy that they feel is lacking in their primary relationships. This yearning can lead them to pursue connections outside of their marriage, driven by unmet emotional needs. However, such deception ultimately results in a breakdown of trust, leaving both partners feeling isolated and betrayed. For the future, fostering an environment where open dialogue about needs, desires, and dissatisfaction is encouraged can help couples address underlying issues before they escalate into infidelity.

Understanding the motivations behind cheating is another crucial aspect that can shape future relationships. Many engage in extramarital affairs out of a desire for excitement, a need for emotional connection, or a response to perceived inadequacies in their primary relationship. Recognizing these motivations can empower individuals to reflect on their own behavior and the state of their primary relationship. By prioritizing self-awareness and empathy, partners can work together to create a more fulfilling and secure bond, reducing the temptation to seek solace outside the marriage.

Moreover, the role of deception in maintaining an extramarital relationship cannot be overlooked. Secrets and lies often serve as the glue that holds these affairs together, but they also sow the seeds of inevitable collapse. The future of relationships must emphasize transparency and integrity, encouraging individuals to confront their actions and the implications they have for all involved. This shift away from deception fosters healthier dynamics, where individuals can engage in honest self-reflection and make informed decisions about their relationships without resorting to betrayal.

In conclusion, the lessons learned from the

realm of deception in extramarital affairs offer valuable insights for anyone navigating the complexities of love. By prioritizing open communication, understanding motivations, and embracing transparency, individuals can cultivate more authentic and fulfilling relationships. The future of relationships hinges on a collective commitment to honesty and emotional connection, allowing love to flourish in its most genuine form. Ultimately, by addressing the psychological aspects of infidelity, we can aspire to build deeper, more resilient bonds that withstand the tests of time and temptation.